The Military History of World War II: Volume 1

EUROPEAN

LAND BATTLES

1939-1943

by Trevor Nevitt Dupuy
COL., U.S. ARMY, RET.

FRANKLIN WATTS, INC.
575 Lexington Avenue • New York 22

To Ernest, who still likes history

4   5   6   7   8

Library of Congress Catalog Card Number: 62-7382
Copyright © 1962 by Franklin Watts, Inc.
Printed in the United States of America

Contents

How World War II Began

The Plan for Conquest

ON NOVEMBER 5, 1937, Adolf Hitler, chancellor and supreme dictator of Nazi Germany, held a secret meeting in the Reichstag. There, behind locked doors, he confided in his foreign ministers and his top military commanders that he was preparing to go to war. He said that Germany was not large enough for its growing population, and that the country needed *Lebensraum* (living space). Since none of Germany's neighbors was likely to give up land without a struggle, the problem of living space for Germany, said Hitler, could be solved only by the use of force. But the use of force must be justified — not only politically but also in the eyes of international law. The conditions that would justify the use of force by Germany must be created before the attack could begin.

Hitler then proceeded to outline the plan for provocations and attacks that he was presently to put into operation. Germany's first objectives would be the conquest of two small neighboring countries, Austria and Czechoslovakia. Of themselves, these would not provide enough territory for the expansion of the German people, but Hitler said that once Austria and Czechoslovakia were under his control it would be easier to absorb the larger and less densely populated regions of Poland and Russia. "It is my unalterable resolve," said Hitler, "to solve Germany's problem of space at the latest by 1943-45." He added that he would act sooner if domestic events in Britain and France presented an opportunity.

Hitler's generals were astonished by these statements. They

1

naturally wished to see their country's strength and influence increased, and they were proud of the fighting qualities of the German army. But they knew that the army was not ready for war against most of the other countries of Europe. They felt that such a war could not be avoided if Hitler went ahead with his plans. And they all remembered clearly how Germany had suffered after 1918, when it was defeated in the terrible four-year struggle of World War I. They urged Hitler not to risk another war like that.

Hitler thought that his generals were too timid. He was sure that Britain, France, and the United States would be so anxious to avoid war that they would not interfere with his plans. He contemptuously rejected his generals' advice and went ahead with his plans.

Four months later — March, 1938 — Hitler began his conquests by sending the German army into Austria and proclaiming that country a part of Germany. There was no opposition. The German generals had been afraid that the invasion of Austria would unite Britain, France, and Soviet Russia in an effort to crush Germany for such flagrant aggression. But these countries did nothing.

The German generals began to wonder if perhaps they had been wrong and Hitler had been right. Then — six months later, in September, 1938 — Hitler won such a great diplomatic triumph that his generals were convinced his plans would work.

Munich

ON SEPTEMBER 29, 1938, four men met at Munich, Germany, to decide whether Europe was to have war or peace. The men were

Adolf Hitler and Prime Minister Benito Mussolini of Italy — dictators who controlled their countries by ruthless police methods — and Prime Minister Neville Chamberlain of England and Premier Édouard Daladier of France — leaders of democratic nations.

The purpose of the meeting was to settle a dispute between Germany and Czechoslovakia. On the Czechoslovak side of the border that separated Czechoslovakia from Germany was a long strip of mountainous country known as the Sudetenland. Before World War I this territory had been part of the old Austro-Hungarian Empire, and most of the people who lived there were of German ancestry. Hitler claimed that the Czechoslovak government was mistreating the Sudeten Germans and threatened to invade the country if the territory was not ceded to Germany at once.

Hitler's charges against Czechoslovakia were false. What he hoped to gain by them was the weakening of his small but sturdy neighbor. It was all part of his plan. Czechoslovakia had a strong army, and all its defenses were in the mountains of the Sudetenland. Hitler knew that if he went to war against France or Russia, Czechoslovakia, allied to both of them, could pose a serious military threat to Germany.

Much had happened in Europe during the twenty years since Germany had been defeated by the Allies in World War I. In 1933, after many years of economic hardship and political unrest in Germany, Adolf Hitler had been appointed chancellor of Germany. Almost immediately he had achieved dictatorial powers. Among his first acts as dictator had been the inauguration of a new economic policy for Germany and the rejection of the provisions of the Versailles Treaty. This treaty after World War I had diminished Germany to a lesser nation by reducing her territory

3

in Europe, stripping her of her colonies in Africa, limiting her production of armaments, and reducing her armed forces. Hitler promised the German people he would restore their country's glory.

In 1934 Hitler had begun to rearm Germany. In 1936 he had marched his troops into the Rhineland, which by the terms of the treaty was to have been occupied by the Allies for fifteen years. In November, 1937, he had held his dramatic meeting with his military leaders, in which he had outlined his plans for conquest in Europe. Then, the following March, had come his easy conquest of Austria.

Meanwhile, the Italian dictator, Mussolini, had dreamed of making Italy as strong as the old Roman Empire. He, too, had increased his country's armed forces and begun to expand his power beyond the borders of his country. In 1935-36, despite the protests of the League of Nations, his armies had invaded and conquered the small, primitive, African country of Ethiopia.

In 1936 Hitler and Mussolini had signed a treaty promising to help each other in case either was attacked. The real purpose of the treaty, however, was to provide mutual aid in the exploitation of small countries as a means of expanding and growing stronger.

The two dictators had called their alliance the Rome-Berlin Axis, and both had hoped that not only France and England but Russia as well would be frightened by their combined military strength. Soon afterwards, Hitler and Mussolini had signed a treaty with the militaristic government of Japan, which was trying to expand its power in Asia. This larger alliance was called the Rome-Berlin-Tokyo Axis.

The growing power of Germany and Italy had alarmed England and France, but the two democracies had not been able to agree

WIDE WORLD PHOTOS

Hitler's troops marching into the Rhineland, 1936.

on joint action, and neither was willing to do anything that might
start a war. Both were reluctant to spend enough money to en-
large their armed forces or to build modern weapons and airplanes. They had hoped that Germany and Italy would not cause
trouble, but they were discovering that to Hitler and Mussolini
weakness was an invitation to aggression.

Since 1937, the two democracies had begun to spend more
money for defense. Both countries were potentially powerful, but
it takes a long time to create strong armies, navies, and air forces.
By 1937 the German army had already become very powerful, and
Hitler was boasting that Germany was the strongest country in

Europe. England and France had believed his boasts. For that reason they had not interfered when he marched into Austria, and for the same reason, on this September day in Munich, they were trying desperately to find a peaceful solution to the dispute between Germany and Czechoslovakia. They did not want to keep their promise, made years earlier, to defend Czechoslovakia in case the little country was attacked.

Russia, too, had promised to defend Czechoslovakia, but Chamberlain and Daladier were so concerned with the weaknesses of the armed forces of their own rich countries that they did not stop to consider how much help they could get from the armies of Russia and Czechoslovakia. Because England and France did not trust the Russian Communists, and because Hitler and Mussolini hated the Russian dictator, Joseph Stalin, Russia had not been invited to the conference. Neither had Czechoslovakia.

Hitler's boasts and threats had been successful. Chamberlain and Daladier were frightened men when they met the German dictator at Munich. They chose to believe him when he said that this would be the last time he would demand territory in Europe. Without even consulting the Czechoslovak leaders, they agreed that Hitler could have the Sudetenland.

PHOTO FROM EUROPEAN

Winston Churchill in 1937.

After Munich

MANY Englishmen agreed with Chamberlain and Daladier that it would have been silly to risk a war over a dispute that concerned neither France nor England. But there were some —led by Winston Churchill — who were dismayed by what had happened. They not only felt it was a disgrace for their country to have helped Hitler take the Sudetenland from their tiny Czechoslovak ally, but they also believed the German dictator had been bluffing about his strength and would have backed down if the democracies had shown themselves willing to fight. They did not believe Hitler's promise of no further territorial demands. They said that Chamberlain and Daladier had achieved not peace but appeasement; that they had only encouraged Hitler to grab more and more territory, until England and France would have to fight or surrender.

Churchill and his friends were right. Six months after Munich, a defenseless Czechoslovakia surrendered to Hitler, who divided the country into several portions, with most of it under the direct control of Germany. A month later, Mussolini sent an army across the Adriatic Sea to seize the little country of Albania. And Hitler began to threaten Poland just as he had threatened Czechoslovakia.

The Polish Dispute

FOR MORE than a century before World War I, Poland had been divided between the German, Russian, and Austrian empires. The Treaty of Versailles had re-established Poland as an independent nation. One part of this new Poland extended north along the Vistula River to the Baltic Sea, cutting off the large German region of

7

East Prussia from the rest of Germany. The German people bitterly resented the fact that their country was split in two by this "Polish Corridor," as it was called.

The city of Danzig, which had been made a free city after World War I, served as Poland's outlet to the Baltic Sea. It was situated on the seacoast border between East Prussia and the Polish Corridor. Danzig had once belonged to Prussia and most of the people were German. Hitler now demanded that the city become part of Germany. He also insisted on the right to build and operate roads and railroads in the Polish Corridor that would connect two parts of Germany.

The English and French governments suddenly awoke to the terrible mistake they had made at Munich. Hurriedly they began to build up their armed forces. Although Germany had become even stronger, Chamberlain promised Poland that if Germany attacked, this time England would fight.

Now, at last, England and France turned to Russia, trying to persuade the Soviet nation to join them in opposing Hitler. They were too late. Stalin, after watching their performance at Munich, had decided he could not trust the democracies, and had made a deal with his hated fellow dictator, Hitler. The two countries, Germany and Russia, had signed a treaty agreeing not to fight each other. And in a secret clause of that treaty, they had agreed to divide Poland between them.

Only Russia could have interfered with a German attack on Poland at that time, and Hitler knew it. He was certain England and France would back down, just as they had at Munich, but even if they did decide to fight, they were too far away to help Poland. Hitler was now ready to start World War II.

CENTRAL EUROPE ON THE EVE OF WORLD WAR II

The Fighting Starts

Blitzkrieg *in Poland*

SHORTLY after midnight on September 1, 1939, fleets of German airplanes began to bomb Polish cities. Just before dawn, five great German armies swept over the Polish frontiers.

Hitler and his generals had planned carefully for this invasion. They had gathered about sixty divisions, consisting of some 1,250,000 men. Nine of these divisions were armored, each having some 150 tanks, and contingents of infantry soldiers who rode to battle in armored trucks and tractors, as well as powerful self-propelled artillery cannon that rumbled over the Polish country-side with the tanks.

The over-all commander of this great invasion force was General Walther von Brauchitsch. In southeast Germany and Slovakia, General Gerd von Rundstedt commanded the three field armies that were crossing the Polish frontiers in that area. In the north, General Fedor von Bock led the two armies that were striking from either side of the Polish Corridor. Supporting the ground troops were about 1,600 planes of the *Luftwaffe*, the German air force.

10

BLITZKRIEG IN POLAND

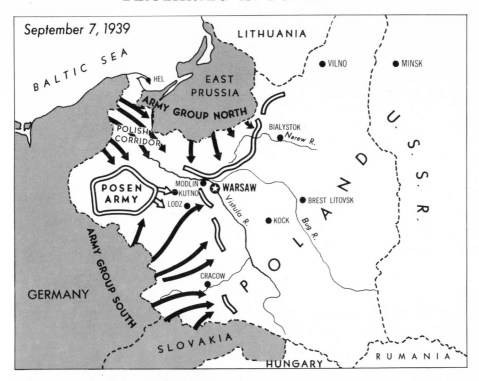

September 7, 1939

BALTIC SEA

LITHUANIA

HEL

EAST PRUSSIA

ARMY GROUP NORTH

POLISH CORRIDOR

BIALYSTOK

Narew R.

MODLIN

KUTNO

WARSAW

LODZ

POSEN ARMY

Vistula R.

BREST LITOVSK

KOCK

Bug R.

CRACOW

GERMANY

ARMY GROUP SOUTH

POLAND

U. S. S. R.

SLOVAKIA

HUNGARY

RUMANIA

VILNO

MINSK

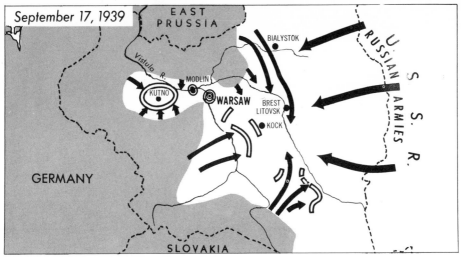

September 17, 1939

EAST PRUSSIA

Vistula R.

MODLIN

KUTNO

WARSAW

BIALYSTOK

BREST LITOVSK

KOCK

RUSSIAN ARMIES

U. S. S. R.

GERMANY

SLOVAKIA

Under the command of Marshal Edward Smigly Rydz, Poland had about 600,000 men ready to fight, and about 2,000,000 trained reserves. But not more than a quarter of the reservists ever got into battle, and few of those who did were in organized units. Before the reserves could be assembled, the *Luftwaffe* had destroyed the Polish railroads, thus preventing mobilization.

The Poles were hardy and they fought bravely, but except for the air force, their equipment was neither as good nor as modern as that of the Germans. There were 500 good planes in the Polish air force, and their pilots were skillful, but most of the Polish planes were destroyed either in the first surprise attacks on the airfields or in follow-up attacks. The few that remained were soon overwhelmed by the superior numbers of German aircraft.

PHOTO FROM EUROPEAN

German troops constructing a ponton bridge over a river in Poland.

The conquest of Czechoslovakia had given the Germans an important advantage: it had enabled them to attack from positions on three sides of western Poland — from Slovakia on the south, Germany on the west, and East Prussia on the north. The Germans planned to use this advantage to make a giant encirclement of the entire Polish army, and the Poles, by trying to defend their country along the western frontiers, unintentionally helped the Germans to carry out their plan.

For four days there was bitter fighting just inside the frontiers of Poland. The defenders fought bravely, but they were severely handicapped. Through their spies and by close aerial observation, the Germans had discovered the location of the Polish general headquarters and had bombed it intensively. Every time it moved, the Germans found it and continued their unmerciful pounding from the air. The Polish defenders were fighting without central direction.

Soon there were gaps in the Polish defenses, and the Germans discovered them. Their armored divisions dashed through the gaps and struck deep behind the Polish lines, adding to the confusion already created by the air attacks. By September 5, all five of the attacking German armies had smashed through the Polish front-line defenses. In the north, Bock's two armies had cut across the Polish Corridor, and his left flank was sending spearheads southward toward Bialystok and Brest Litovsk. In the extreme south, the German right-flank army was streaming eastward past Cracow.

The most spectacular advances were made by the central army of Rundstedt's wing. This army, commanded by General Walther von Reichenau, had been given most of the German armored divisions. By September 8, Reichenau's tanks had reached the outskirts of Warsaw and were actually trying to drive into the Polish capital.

13

PHOTO FROM EUROPEAN

The stubborn resistance of the defenders of Warsaw gave temporary hope to the Polish people and their British and French allies. The German tanks were repulsed, and a few miles to the west, between Kutno and Lodz, Polish counterattacks halted the advance of Rundstedt's left-flank army. For six days a violent battle raged around Kutno, but it was an uneven contest. German reinforcements forced the Poles to halt their attacks, and the Germans resumed their advance, encircling the Polish defenders at Lodz and Kutno. Under incessant air and ground attack, and cut off from all supplies and reinforcements, 170,000 Polish troops surrendered on September 17.

Meanwhile, the German flank armies had completed their encirclement. The spearheads met just south of Brest Litovsk. The Polish high command now tried to withdraw the remnants of its armies to southeastern Poland in order to establish a new defensive line. They prepared to smash their way through the thin line of encircling Germans, but before they could get started, new German spearheads had created another line of encirclement.

Two bands of steel now cut off the main Polish armies from their headquarters in the southeast of Poland. And as if this were not enough, on September 17 Russia invaded Poland from the east. The few Polish units not hemmed in by the Germans were soon overwhelmed by the Russians. The Polish government and high command gave up their attempt to organize a last-ditch resistance in southeastern Poland. On September 18 they took refuge in Romania.

The scattered Polish units in central Poland fought on heroically,

A German armored division parading after the invasion of Poland.

15

but there was little they could do against the might of the victorious German army. One by one they were bombed or starved
into submission. Warsaw fell on September 27; the fortress city of
Modlin yielded on September 28; the Polish naval base of Hel, on
the Baltic, capitulated on October 1. The surrender of the last organized Polish unit took place at Kock, on October 5.

The Poles had lost about 66,000 men killed and at least 200,000
wounded, while the remainder of their army of a million men had
been captured. The cost to Germany had been only 10,000 men
killed and 30,000 wounded. It was one of the most thorough and
stunning victories in the history of warfare.

The secret of the German victory in Poland lay in the way in
which the Germans made use of their modern weapons — partic-
ularly their tanks and aircraft. Their teamwork was perfect. They
would strike small areas with overwhelming numbers of infantry,
artillery, and aircraft, quickly punching holes in the Polish lines.
Then the tanks would race through, far into the Polish rear, while
bombers struck even farther back, cutting roads and railroads,
breaking telegraph lines. Time and again the Germans did this.
No matter where the Poles turned, or how bravely they fought,

WIDE WORLD PHOTOS

*German infantrymen ad-
vancing through barbed
wire entanglements on the
outskirts of Warsaw.*

WIDE WORLD PHOTOS

German troops in Warsaw trying to dislodge Polish snipers who continued to harass them even after the city was conquered.

the Germans were soon upon them, slashing from side, front, and rear, cutting off food and supplies. The Polish armies were paralyzed.

This was not really a new way of making war. Great generals of the past had won victories in similar fashion. But they had not had tanks or aircraft or motorized infantry at their command, as Hitler did. The Germans rightly compared their fighting method to the speed and power of lightning. They called it *Blitzkrieg* — "lightning war."

Sitzkrieg *in Western Europe*

WHILE the fighting raged in Poland, a strange situation existed in western Europe. Although England and France, carrying out their promise to Poland, had declared war against Germany on September 3, the spirit that had led to appeasement at Munich still gov-

While the French watched from their Maginot Line, the Germans finished building tank impediments on their Siegfried Line.

WIDE WORLD PHOTOS

German anti-aircraft emplacements on the Siegfried Line.

WIDE WORLD PHOTOS

-WIDE WORLD PHOTOS

Underground tunnel on the Maginot Line. Double-track railways led to ammunition dumps and elevators serving gun stations.

WIDE WORLD PHOTOS

Tank barricades on the Maginot Line.

erned the actions of the two countries. French soldiers sat in their
trenches, either unwilling or unable to help their Polish allies.
Hitler had less than 400,000 men holding the half-finished Siegfried Line, or *Westwall,* which he had begun a few years earlier
in answer to France's Maginot Line, the powerful chain of fortifications extending along the border region opposite Germany.
But despite the weakness of the German defenses, neither France
nor England was prepared to invade Germany. In contrast to the
war in Poland, observers called this the *Sitzkrieg,* the "sit-down
war."

The Russo-Finnish War

DESPITE the fact that they had signed a treaty dividing Poland between their two countries, Hitler and Stalin continued to distrust each other. Stalin, who would not have hesitated to attack Germany if he had thought he could win, was quite certain that Hitler was planning to attack Russia. Germany was stronger than Russia in 1939, so Stalin decided he had better do whatever he could to strengthen his own country. If Hitler was going to attack Russia, Stalin was going to make it as difficult for him as possible.

The Russian dictator was worried about the growing strength of the German navy in the Baltic Sea. The long arm of the Baltic called the Gulf of Finland led right to Leningrad, Russia's second-largest city. To the southwest of this important manufacturing center lay the three tiny Baltic countries of Estonia, Latvia, and Lithuania. The republic of Finland held the north shore of the Gulf of Finland, right up to the outskirts of Leningrad.

Stalin first demanded that Estonia, Latvia, and Lithuania permit Russian troops to occupy army and naval bases in their countries. With the Russian army massed on their frontiers, the governments of these three countries knew they were helpless. On October 10, 1939, they agreed to let the Russians come in without fighting. This meant the end of freedom for the Baltic States.

Next, on October 14, Stalin demanded that Finland give up some important military bases on the north shore of the Gulf of Finland. Russian soldiers in great numbers were assembled along the border between Finland and Russia.

The population of Russia was about 200 million; that of Finland, only four million. But the Finns were too proud to give up national territory under a Russian threat. They rejected Stalin's demand even when he rushed a tremendous army to the border and threatened to invade the tiny country.

On November 30, without even declaring war, Stalin sent his planes to bomb the Finnish cities of Helsinki and Viipuri. He thought this would frighten the Finns into giving in. It did nothing of the kind. The Finns shot back at the Russian planes, and Stalin ordered his armies to attack.

Finland, however, was prepared. The Finnish army had made careful plans for fighting a defensive war. The troops were well trained and equipped for winter warfare. A powerful line of fortifications had been built across the Karelian Isthmus, the neck of land between the Gulf of Finland and Lake Ladoga, where ran the only good roads connecting Russia with Finland. These fortifications were called the Mannerheim Line, after Baron Carl von Mannerheim, the capable commanding general of the Finnish army.

While the Russians threatened, the Finns had been quietly mobilizing their reserves. By the time Russia attacked, the Finns had 400,000 men under arms — an amazing number for such a small country. There was a strong garrison in the Mannerheim Line, and all along the Russian frontier in the east were a number of light, well-equipped, well-trained divisions of ski troops.

On November 30, five Russian armies — nearly 500,000 men —

PHOTO FROM EUROPEAN

Finnish gunners in action on the Russian border.

23

attacked all along the Russian-Finnish frontier. At the start, a "fifth column" of Finnish communists began making trouble behind the lines in Finland. The Russians were sure that the combination of air attacks, massed army invasion, and fifth column activity would bring the Finns to their knees.

Again the Russians were wrong. The Finnish police and home guard took care of the fifth column. Bad December weather hampered the Russian air attacks. And the Finns cut the Russian army to pieces.

At Suomussalmi, in east central Finland, one understrength Finnish division completely destroyed two Russian divisions. North of Lake Ladoga, another Russian division was captured. All of the Russian attacks on the eastern frontier were driven back. All along the Mannerheim Line so many Russians were killed that the Finnish defenders became sick from the slaughter.

By the end of December the Russians had abandoned their attacks. For the next month they revised their plans and collected even larger forces. They decided they would concentrate everything they had against the Mannerheim Line.

The renewed Russian attack began February 1, 1940, with a terrific bombardment. On February 13, after terrible losses, the Russians broke through the line. The Finns now knew they could not win, and so they made peace with the Russians. The fighting stopped on March 13. Finland had to give up the Karelian Isthmus and some bases on the Gulf of Finland, as well as Petsamo on the Arctic Ocean.

Finland had lost the war, but the little country had shown the world a display of national courage rarely equaled in history. Finnish losses were 18,000 killed and 42,000 wounded. The Russians have never disclosed their casualties, but they were probably about 150,000 killed and more than 300,000 wounded.

24

The Campaign in Norway

WHILE Russia was fighting Finland, the *Sitzkrieg* continued along the border between France and Germany. French soldiers in the Maginot Line watched while the Germans busily continued their construction of the Siegfried Line. But out of sight of the Allies, Hitler was preparing for a second *Blitzkrieg*. The victims this time were to be Norway and Denmark.

Hitler had three reasons for wanting to control Norway. First, most of the iron that Germany used in its industry came from northern Sweden. The ore was shipped by rail to Narvik, in Norway, and then by boat along the coast of Norway to Germany. This iron was absolutely essential to the German war machine. Hitler was afraid that the British navy might interfere with the shipments along the coast of Norway — and the British navy was preparing to do just that.

In the second place, Hitler wanted to control Norway so that he could break the British naval blockade of Germany. Britain had successfully cut off all Germany's overseas trade by patrolling the English Channel and the other entrances to the narrow North Sea, which lies between Germany, Britain, and Norway. But with the long coast of Norway under German control, the British would have a very difficult time maintaining a tight blockade. On the

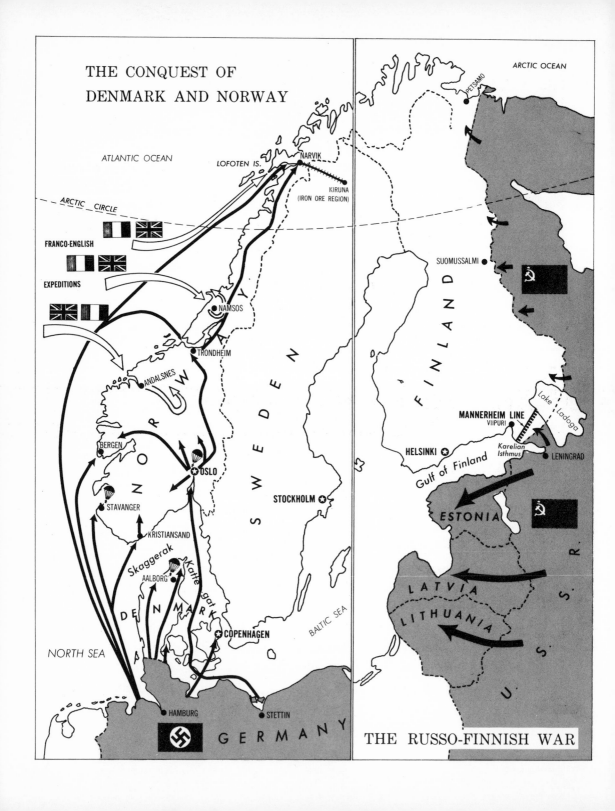

THE CONQUEST OF
DENMARK AND NORWAY

ATLANTIC OCEAN

LOFOTEN IS.

NARVIK

ARCTIC CIRCLE

KIRUNA
(IRON ORE REGION)

FRANCO-ENGLISH

EXPEDITIONS

NAMSOS

TRONDHEIM

ANDALSNES

S
W
E
D
E
N

N
O
R
W
A
Y

BERGEN

OSLO

STAVANGER

STOCKHOLM

KRISTIANSAND

Skaggerak

Kattegat

AALBORG

D
E
N
M
A
R
K

COPENHAGEN

BALTIC SEA

NORTH SEA

HAMBURG

STETTIN

GERMANY

ARCTIC OCEAN

PETSAMO

SUOMUSSALMI

F
I
N
L
A
N
D

Lake Ladoga

MANNERHEIM LINE
VIIPURI

HELSINKI

Karelian Isthmus

LENINGRAD

Gulf of Finland

ESTONIA

U. S. S. R.

LATVIA

LITHUANIA

THE RUSSO-FINNISH WAR

other hand, it would be easy for German warships and submarines based in Norway to get out into the Atlantic to attack ships bringing supplies to England and France.

Finally, control of Norway would give Germany good air bases for long-range air attacks and observation flights over England and Scotland.

Hitler's chief reason for wanting Denmark was to make it easier for German ships and soldiers to get to Norway. But the capture of Denmark would also give Germany control over the sea routes leading into and out of the Baltic Sea through the narrow straits of the Skagerrak and Kattegat.

The British had no idea that Hitler was planning to invade Norway, but they did know how important the Swedish ore shipments were to Germany. They had made plans to lay a large mine field along the Norwegian coast, even though Norway was a neutral country. April 8, 1940, was the date set for the beginning of the British mine-laying operation — April 9 was the day the Germans had chosen for their surprise attack against Norway.

The German attack was to be made against six Norwegian seaports — Oslo (capital of Norway), Kristiansand, Stavanger, Bergen, Trondheim, and Narvik. About 150,000 soldiers, under the command of General Nikolaus von Falkenhorst, would take part in this operation. Most of them were already on their way to Norway by sea, some on German warships, but most in empty iron-ore barges the Germans were pretending to return to Narvik. Other soldiers would be transported by air after parachutists had seized the main Norwegian airfields.

While they prepared their attack on Norway, the Germans had been trying to frighten the Norwegian people into submission. The German ambassador had invited leading Norwegian citizens

FYLKESBILENE I NORD-TRØNDELAG
HOLDEPLASS

PHOTO FROM EUROPEAN

The harbor of Namsos after German bombers were through with it. The sign in the foreground was all that remained of a public garage.

to watch moving pictures of the devastating German ground and air attacks against the armies and cities of Poland. The Germans hoped these would do the trick, but in case the Norwegians did try to resist, the Germans had been foresighted enough to organize a well-prepared fifth column under a Norwegian named Vidkun Quisling.

On April 8, the German navy was out in force to protect the troop convoys on their way to Norway. On that same day the British fleet came in close to Norway to lay its mines. The result was a series of hard-fought naval engagements along the entire Norwegian coast. The British sank several German warships and lost a few of their own, but they failed to discover the troop transports the German navy was protecting.

Early next morning the Germans attacked. They invaded and conquered Denmark in one day, almost without a shot's being fired. But it was not quite so easy in Norway.

Norway had worried more about the British mine field than about any possibility of German attack. The invasion was a complete surprise to the small, unprepared Norwegian armed forces.

Grim-faced Norwegian troops crossing a bridge in a truck on their way to the front lines.

PHOTO FROM EUROPEAN

Norwegian patriots, ready to sacrifice their lives, destroyed large quantities of German supplies passing through the railroad tunnels. Here German troops are shown in one of the armored cars used to shoot down saboteurs.

PHOTO FROM EUROPEAN

Norwegian ski patrol.

But the Norwegians had one advantage, and that was their geographic position. The Germans could get at them only by an overseas attack. And so, fighting desperately, they were able to interfere with the German operations. Several German ships were sunk, and many men were killed by the Norwegian army and navy coast-defense forces. The German attack against Oslo was slowed, and King Haakon and his government were able to get out of the city before the German troops overwhelmed its defenders.

In spite of the delays, the Germans were successful everywhere they attacked. Quickly they pushed inland while the German air force flew great quantities of supplies to the airfields at the captured seaports. It was important for the Germans to establish an overland link between Trondheim and southern Norway as soon as possible, for the British navy was certain to interfere with

PHOTO FROM EUROPEAN

WIDE WORLD PHOTOS

32

German supply column advancing in the Norwegian mountains.

any supply transports that tried to reach Norway's western seaports.

The British and French reacted quickly to Germany's invasion of Norway. While the Germans were brushing aside the Norwegian army without too much trouble, about 30,000 Allied troops were landed at Namsos and Aandalsnes, north and south of Trondheim. They hoped to be able to surround and hold Trondheim before the Germans from the south could arrive. Meanwhile, other Allied troops were on their way to try to recapture Narvik from the Germans.

But the Germans were much better prepared than the Allies. By May 1 they had massed more than 80,000 troops near Trondheim. The British and French troops who had set out to defend the city were forced back on the defensive. As the German pressure increased, the British navy had to take the defeated Allied soldiers back to England. The king of Norway and his government also escaped to England. By May 5, the Germans were in complete control of southern Norway. At Narvik the struggle continued for another month, but by June 9 the last Allied soldiers were also withdrawn from northern Norway.

The Allied effort in Norway had been "too little and too late." The Germans had captured two more countries with the same speed and efficiency they had shown in Poland. Hitler had accomplished his purpose. Norway was very useful to him for the remainder of the war.

Germany Invades the West

German and Allied Plans

EVEN WHILE the invasion of Norway was taking place, the Germans were preparing for a larger operation. Hitler felt sure that his army was strong enough now to win a great victory and force the Allies to make peace. He had decided to attack the French and British armies in France.

In western Germany Hitler assembled 104 infantry divisions, 8 motorized divisions, and 10 armored divisions — about 2,500,000 men. Opposite Holland, Field Marshal von Bock held ready an army group of two field armies. Stretched along the border between France and Germany, facing the Maginot Line, was Field Marshal von Leeb's group of two armies. In the center, massed next to the frontiers of Belgium and Luxembourg was the army group of Field Marshal von Rundstedt, consisting of six field armies. This was the main striking force, and had most of the armored divisions. Over-all commander of this great force was Field Marshal von Brauchitsch, who had commanded the invasion forces in Poland.

The French and British armies combined were only slightly smaller than the German force assembling for invasion, but they were less well trained and equipped. And the French, in particular, lacked the confidence and fighting spirit of the Germans. Although they had almost as many tanks as the Germans, the French had only three armored divisions. The rest of their tanks were scattered through the remaining ninety infantry, fortress, and cavalry divisions of the French army.

Half of the French army was in or near the Maginot Line. The other half, plus the ten divisions of the British Expeditionary Force, was located near the Belgian border of France. The overall commander of the Allied armies was French General Maurice Gamelin. General Lord Gort commanded the British army under Gamelin.

In addition to these Allied forces, Belgium had a total of about 600,000 soldiers organized in twenty-two divisions, but they were poorly trained and equipped. There was also a Dutch army of about 400,000 men, even less well prepared for war than the Belgians. Belgium and Holland were neutral countries, and they were most eager to avoid being forced into the war. So as not to provoke Hitler, they were very careful not to make any joint plans for defense with the British and French. Even when the German armies began to mass opposite their frontiers, Belgian and Dutch military leaders refused to consult with the Allied generals.

The Allies were sure that Hitler would advance through Holland and Belgium to avoid an attack against the Maginot Line. The Allied high command, therefore, prepared a plan to help the Low Countries if they were attacked. The main French and British armies would advance to the Dyle River in Belgium. The Allies called this plan "Plan D."

WIDE WORLD PHOTOS

German troops crossing the Maas River on an improvised bridge at Maastricht, Holland.

The Germans knew that there were no agreed plans between the French and British on the one hand, and the Dutch and Belgians on the other. But they guessed correctly that the French and British would try to help the Low Countries in the way outlined in Plan D. To encourage the British and French to rush northward, the Germans planned to make their first heavy attacks against Holland and northern Belgium.

After the Allies had gotten well into the Low Countries, the main force of Rundstedt's army group planned to strike through the Ardennes Forest of southern Belgium and cut straight through the middle of the Allied armies. The Germans were sure that the Allies would not expect an attack across this wooded, mountainous country where marching and fighting were so difficult. And they were certain that the Allies would not expect the main German tank forces to go through the Ardennes. The Germans had studied the ground and the roads carefully. They believed they could get through the region so quickly that they would be in northern France before the Allies could change their plans and move troops to block the narrow roads of the difficult Ardennes.

The Attack on Holland and Belgium

BEFORE dawn on May 10, the *Luftwaffe* made widespread bombing attacks over Belgium and Holland. Just after dawn German paratroopers landed near Rotterdam and The Hague in Holland. They seized key bridges over the wide Waal (Rhine) and Maas

(Meuse) rivers while German armies struck deep into both Holland and Belgium. The Dutch and the Belgians were completely unprepared for the German *Blitzkrieg*. They were driven back in great confusion all along the line.

As the Germans had expected, the French and British immediately put Plan D into operation and began to advance into Belgium and Holland. But this did not stop the German attacks. While the Dutch army reeled back, the Germans destroyed the center of Rotterdam with a brutal bombing attack. They threatened to make more such attacks if the Dutch did not surrender. Queen Wilhelmina and the Dutch government fled by ship to

German parachute troops in front of the fort of Eben-Emael, shortly after the fort's surrender.

PHOTO FROM EUROPEAN

Britain, where they joined the Norwegian government-in-exile. The Dutch army surrendered on May 14.

The Belgians had hoped to stop any German invasion along the line of the wide Albert Canal in eastern Belgium. The key to the defenses covering this canal was a powerful fortress called Fort Eben Emael. On the very first day of the invasion German troop-carrying gliders landed on top of the fort and attacked its gun turrets and air vents. By May 11 the fort was in German hands, and the entire Belgian defense plan had been ruined. The discouraged Belgian soldiers fell back to the Dyle River to join the Allies.

Breakthrough in the Ardennes

THE ARMORED and infantry divisions of Rundstedt spent three days pushing their way through the wooded hills of the Ardennes, but by the evening of May 12 they had crossed the French border and reached the Meuse River at Sedan and Mézières. The French were completely surprised. They had only a thin line of soldiers to face the Germans. General Gamelin tried to bring back some of his troops from northern and central Belgium, and sent for additional reinforcements from other parts of France.

But the French reinforcements could not get there in time to help. By the evening of May 13 the leading German infantry divisions had driven across the Meuse and built several pontoon bridges. Across these bridges German tanks, guns, and infantry poured in a never-ending stream night and day. By the evening of May 15 the Germans had blasted a gap fifty miles wide in the French line. German armored spearheads had begun to drive ahead, just as they had done in Poland.

WIDE WORLD PHOTOS

A German field artillery detachment on the advance in Holland.

Flanders and the Somme River

BY THE TIME French and British troops began to return from the Low Countries, it was too late to plug the hole in the French lines. The Germans were driving ahead relentlessly toward the English Channel. Their spearheads raced down the Somme River valley.

40

Only twice did the Germans run into serious opposition. On May 17 their spearheads were thrown back briefly by a French armored counterattack led by General Charles de Gaulle. But De Gaulle had no infantry support, and he was forced finally to withdraw. The same thing happened on May 19. After that day's

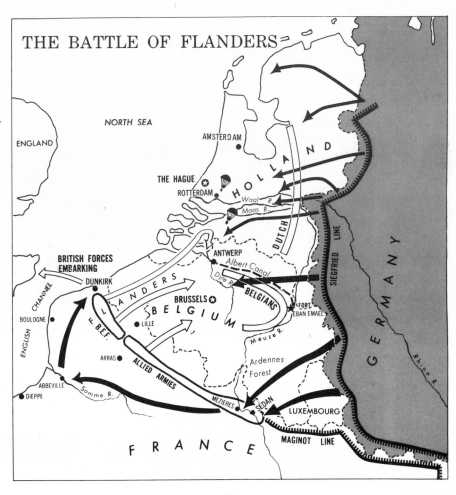

THE BATTLE OF FLANDERS

battle, De Gaulle had too few tanks left to attack again.

Early on May 21, the armored division commanded by German General Erwin Rommel reached the English Channel near Abbeville. By now a corridor of German tanks and infantry had cut the Allied forces completely in two. About half of the Allies were south of the German corridor. The other half were in Flanders — the northern tip of France and southwestern Belgium.

Later on that same day the Germans reached the French seaport of Boulogne, the main supply base of the British army. Here they were halted briefly by a small force of British defenders.

German troops crossing a Belgian river in a small rubber boat.

WIDE WORLD PHOTOS

The Allied forces at this time were commanded by an aging hero of World War I, General Maxime Weygand, who had replaced General Gamelin. Weygand planned to have the troops in Flanders and those in France attack the German corridor simultaneously. The French managed to advance slightly in the south, but the Germans quickly drove them back. In Flanders, the British and the French were trying to hold off the Germans who were driving against them through Holland and Belgium. They were being pushed so hard they could not attempt a counterattack in the opposite direction against the German corridor.

The Allied troops in Belgium and Flanders were the best of the British and French armies. They fought well against intensifying German pressure, and for a while they managed to halt the advance. But the ill-prepared Belgian troops were nearly helpless. By May 27 they had been so badly cut up that King Leopold surrendered the entire Belgian army to the Germans.

There was no hope now of holding any part of Flanders. The British troops were pressed back almost to the sea near Dunkirk, and the British Royal Navy was preparing to take them off the Continent.

Dunkirk

THE EVACUATION vessels that the Royal Navy was collecting off the coast of France were an amazing flotilla of every possible kind of ship or boat that could be found along the coasts of southern England. In addition to warships there were yachts, tugboats, ferryboats, and even small motorboats. Every Englishman who owned any kind of seaworthy craft, or who could help to sail one, joined in this great national effort.

On May 28, while some of the British and French soldiers held off the German attacks, the first British soldiers waded out into the water to be picked up by the vessels arriving from England.

The Germans relaxed their pressure on the retreating Allies. Hitler had ordered the German army not to push so hard because he wanted the German air force to share in the glory by smashing the British as they tried to get on their ships.

But the Royal Air Force, based in nearby Britain, was at last able to get into the fight. It kept the *Luftwaffe* so busy that there were not many German air attacks against the British soldiers on the crowded beaches or on the mass of ships and boats waiting to take the men on board.

By June 2, when Hitler realized his mistake, it was too late. The last of 225,000 British and 112,000 French soldiers had been taken on the British vessels and brought to England. The Royal Navy, however, had lost several destroyers to German bombing attacks.

Allied troops, under German bombardment, file through the town of Dunkirk on their way to the beaches.

WIDE WORLD PHOTOS

WIDE WORLD PHOTOS

These were among the oddly assorted craft that crossed the channel from England to evacuate Allied troops from Dunkirk.

The success of the Dunkirk evacuation was only a tiny bright spot in a very gloomy picture. Counting the Belgians and the Dutch, nearly 2,000,000 Allied soldiers had been put out of action in about three weeks. And even though the evacuation of Dunkirk had been a success, here, too, the Allies had suffered a serious loss. The troops had had to leave all of their guns, trucks, tanks, and other heavy equipment behind them.

The British and French hurriedly tried to get ready for further

45

attacks, but there was little hope that they could stop the victorious German army. Most of the French, and probably more than half of the British, were sure they would be completely defeated by the Germans.

There was one Englishman, however, who refused to think of defeat. On May 10, the British nation had called on Winston Churchill to replace Neville Chamberlain as prime minister. Unlike Chamberlain, who had promised the English "peace in our time," Churchill did not minimize the dangers that lay ahead for England. He told the people, "I have nothing to offer but blood, toil, tears, and sweat."

The British people united behind Winston Churchill. It was he who had inspired the tremendous national effort that resulted in the "Miracle of Dunkirk." And now, early in June, 1940, he was hastily trying to scrape up weapons to give to the men who had come back. He was determined that England — and France too, if possible — win the war.

Allied troops wading into the surf to board the craft that carried them from the beaches of Dunkirk to safety in England.

WIDE WORLD PHOTOS

The Battle of France

The French Collapse

JUNE OF 1940 found General Weygand faced with a problem for which there seemed no solution. He had lost most of his best troops when they were cut off in Flanders, and few of the men who had been evacuated at Dunkirk would be able to return soon enough to join the battle that might start at any moment. With less than 1,500,000 discouraged men, Weygand had to face an expected attack by 2,500,000 victorious Germans. And for more than 150 miles — from the end of the Maginot Line to the English Channel — his men had no prepared defenses to help them stop the Germans.

The Germans gave the French no time to prepare any extensive field fortifications or entrenchments. On June 5 they renewed the attack.

For several days the French line held firm, though the Germans dented it in a few places. But the French were spread out too thin, and they began to give way. On June 12 the Germans broke through the French lines east of Reims. Other breakthroughs followed in rapid succession. Armored spearheads stabbed into the French countryside.

One armored force, quickly followed by infantry, drove to the frontier of Switzerland, cutting off the Maginot Line from the rest of France. The garrisons of these fortifications had been greatly weakened because Weygand had had to take men from them to strengthen the lines south of the Somme River.

Now that they had surrounded the entire area of the Maginot Line, the Germans began to attack from all directions, but with their main effort from the rear. They used paratroopers and small teams of infantry and engineers to attack and blow up some of the separate gun emplacements. Completely disheartened, the French defenders surrendered.

The main German attack swept through and around Paris. The French government and army had evacuated their capital on June 13, declaring it an open city to keep it from being destroyed. By June 17 the German tanks had reached the Loire River at Orléans. Streams of civilian refugees, trying to escape the swift German advance, clogged the French roads. It was almost impossible for the defending army to move troops to stem the tide.

Meanwhile, on June 10, Italy had declared war on France. Mussolini had wanted to be sure to get into the war in time to claim some of the French and English colonies. But the French defenders of the Alps, even though they were outnumbered, were able to hold off the Italian attacks.

In central France, however, it was clear that nothing could stop the Germans. Churchill flew to France to persuade Premier Paul Reynaud to move the French government to Algeria and carry on the war there, but it was too late. The French had suffered more than a defeat of arms. They had lost the will and the desire to fight. Although Reynaud wanted to follow Churchill's advice, other Frenchmen, led by aged Marshal Henri Pétain, hero of World War

48

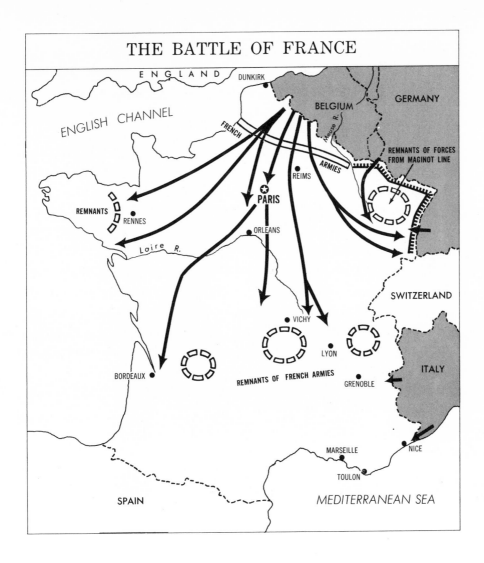

THE BATTLE OF FRANCE

I, and the politician Pierre Laval, insisted that France surrender. Reynaud resigned, and Pétain became premier. Immediately he offered to make peace, and Churchill returned despondently to England.

On June 21, the French signed an armistice in the same railroad car that had witnessed the German surrender at the close of World War I. On June 25, just after midnight, the fighting stopped.

The Germans now occupied most of France, but they allowed the French government to stay in existence in the small city of Vichy. From there Pétain went through the motions of governing the French colonies and part of southern France. Actually he was little more than a figurehead in a government completely dominated by Hitler. It was his vice-premier, Pierre Laval, lawyer, politician, and collaborator with the Nazis, who really ran the government, and he ran it exactly as Hitler told him to. Shrewdly, by permitting part of France to remain in existence under its own government, the German dictator had gained another one of his objectives — control of the French colonies.

This picture, found on the body of a dead German soldier, shows French infantrymen massing an attack against the invading Germans.

BIRNBACK PUBLISHING SERVIC

WIDE WORLD PHOTOS

French refugees clogged the roads, impeding troop and supply movements.

Britain Stands Alone

LEAVING Nazi soldiers to hold France under control, the main German armies moved northward to concentrate near the Strait of Dover. Hitler was planning to invade England, which lay just across that narrow stretch of water. While his soldiers rested from their battles, his air force prepared to sweep the British Royal Air Force from the skies.

The German attack on England was expected at any moment, and hardly anyone outside of England thought that the British

KEYSTONE VIEW CO. *Pierre Laval.*

could hold out more than a few weeks. But Churchill had spoken for the British people when, just before the collapse of France, he had said: "We shall not flag or fail. We shall fight in France, we shall fight on the seas and oceans, we shall fight with growing confidence and growing strength in the air, we shall defend our island, whatever the cost may be, we shall fight on the beaches, we shall fight on the landing grounds, we shall fight in the fields and in the streets, we shall fight in the hills; we shall never surrender."

Now, when Britain stood completely alone, he told his people and the world: "Let us therefore brace ourselves to our duties, and so bear ourselves that, if the British Empire and its Commonwealth last for a thousand years, men will still say: 'This was their finest hour.'"

52

PHOTO FROM EUROPEAN

General Charles de Gaulle reviewing a Free French commando unit in England.

The Balkan Campaigns

The Italo-Greek War

ALTHOUGH there had been clashes between Italian and British troops along the Libyan-Egyptian border and in Somaliland, Mussolini could boast of no victories equal to those of Hitler in Poland, Flanders, and France. So, Mussolini thought he would do a little conquering on his own. He decided to start with Greece. From that country he could threaten all the British bases in the eastern Mediterranean area. He thought it would be easy to over-run the tiny country from Albania, which Italy had seized in 1939.

On October 28, 1940, an Italian army of 162,000 men, commanded by General Visconti-Prasca, advanced from Albania into Greece. The Greek army, commanded by General Alexander Papagos, numbered only 150,000 — poorly equipped but tough, well-trained soldiers. In less than three weeks they had completely stopped the Italian invasion, before it had penetrated more than a few miles into Greece. The Greeks were helped by a few squadrons of the British Royal Air Force — all that the British could spare from their battles against the Italians in Africa.

54

Before the end of November, the Greeks counterattacked in the inland mountains, inflicting a severe defeat on the Italian left flank. Then they struck along the rocky seacoast. By early December they had not only driven the Italians out of Greece, but were actually invading Italian-held Albania.

Mussolini rushed reinforcements to Albania, but the Greek advance continued. The Greeks held about one fourth of the country before the strengthened Italian defenders could stop them. The war in Albania was stalemated; neither side could drive the other back.

Italian army engineers repairing a road destroyed by Greek patriots.

WIDE WORLD PHOTOS

German Invasion of the Balkans

HITLER had no desire to help Mussolini out of his troubles in Greece and Albania, but he was worried about the British air bases in Greece. Like Mussolini, he thought it would be wise to use Greece as a base against the British in the Mediterranean. Furthermore, he had decided to invade Russia, and he wanted to make sure that there would be no trouble in the Balkans to interfere with that undertaking.

Early in 1941, Hitler prepared to invade Greece. He began by putting pressure on the governments of Yugoslavia, Hungary, Romania, and Bulgaria. He promised these countries that they would get parts of Greece or Russia if they would join him — he also promised to destroy them if they failed to cooperate.

Once more the German ambassadors unreeled their films of Hitler's victorious campaigns. The Yugoslavs, the Romanians, the Bulgarians, and the Hungarians watched the German Stuka dive bombers smash Warsaw and Rotterdam. In addition, they were treated to the filmed record of the work of the German fifth columns in Norway, Belgium, and France.

The government leaders of the four Balkan countries were so thoroughly frightened that they signed the treaties Hitler put in front of them. Henceforth the German dictator could force them to do whatever he wanted.

The British were greatly disturbed over what had happened in the Balkans. Hurriedly they recalled about 60,000 troops from Africa, where they had just won a great victory over the Italians. By the end of March these troops, under the command of General Henry Wilson, were beginning to take positions on the threatened northeastern frontier of Greece. At the same time, large German

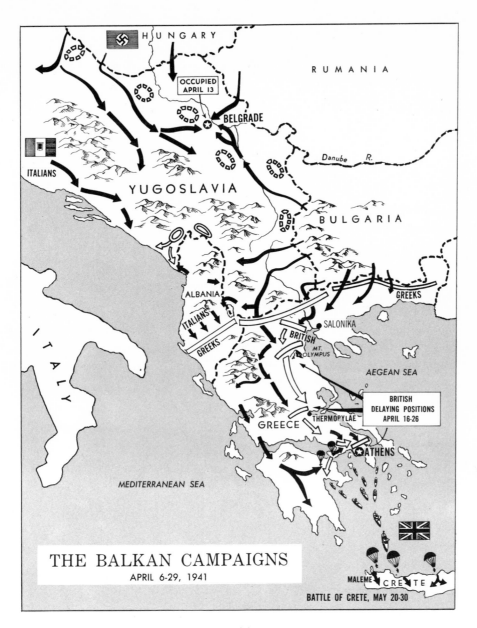

RUMANIA

HUNGARY

OCCUPIED
APRIL 13

BELGRADE

Danube R.

ITALIANS

YUGOSLAVIA

BULGARIA

ALBANIA

GREEKS

ITALIANS

GREEKS

SALONIKA

BRITISH

MT. OLYMPUS

AEGEAN SEA

ITALY

BRITISH
DELAYING POSITIONS
APRIL 16-26

GREECE

THERMOPYLAE

ATHENS

MEDITERRANEAN SEA

THE BALKAN CAMPAIGNS
APRIL 6-29, 1941

MALEME   CRETE

BATTLE OF CRETE, MAY 20-30

forces were beginning to gather in Bulgaria. The German attack on Greece was scheduled for April 6.

Then suddenly the Balkan situation changed. The Yugoslav people rose and threw out the government which had signed the treaty with Germany.

Quickly the German general staff changed its plans. Troops that had been gathering in Hungary, Poland, and eastern Germany for the invasion of Russia were suddenly shifted to the frontiers of Yugoslavia. In less than a week the Germans were ready to attack both Greece and Yugoslavia at the same time.

Hitler's big guns on the march.

WIDE WORLD PHOTOS

WIDE WORLD PHOTOS

German Alpine troops in the mountains of Greece.

Moving the men and supplies to make such an attack in so short a time was an amazing accomplishment.

On April 6 the German air force and army struck Yugoslavia. The stories of Poland, Flanders, and France were repeated. Though the Yugoslavs fought bravely, they were quickly overwhelmed. By April 15, the fighting was almost completely over. The last remaining portion of the Yugoslav army surrendered two days later.

Meanwhile, following the original plan, German troops in Bulgaria had begun the invasion of northeastern Greece on April 6. By April 9 they had driven across the narrow arm of northeastern

Greece to reach the Aegean Sea. They were now facing the British troops in position west of Salonika. The speed of the German tank movements in the rugged Balkan Mountains amazed military men around the world.

A German armored sweep through southern Yugoslavia soon threatened the left flank of the British, who were forced to fall back to a new line in front of Mount Olympus. The British carried out their withdrawal smoothly, but the Greeks on their left flank ran into trouble. The left flank of the Greek army was still facing the Italians in Albania, but the right flank could not stand up against the German attack that was driving between the Greek and British armies.

The British, in strong defensive positions, held the Germans off without difficulty, but they had to fall back again when the Germans smashed through the Greek positions in central Greece. This time General Wilson chose a position near the famous Pass of Thermopylae, but it was clear now that the Greeks could not be rallied. The entire British army was in danger of being cut off and destroyed. General Papagos offered to hold out for as long as he could while the British Royal Navy attempted to take the British troops off the peninsula.

The evacuation began at Athens on April 22. The next day the Greeks were forced to surrender, and the British fell back toward the southern tip of Greece. The Royal Navy's ships could not come in to shore during the daytime because of the strength of the German air force, but every night they came in to take off more soldiers. During the night of April 28-29 the last British soldiers were evacuated. The next day the Germans completed their occupation of the Greek peninsula.

Like the soldiers at Dunkirk, the men evacuated from Greece

WIDE WORLD PHOTOS

German anti-aircraft gun in action on the Grecian front.

had to leave all their guns and heavy equipment on shore for the Germans to capture. The ships that took them off the peninsula had taken terrible punishment from the *Luftwaffe*. But once more the Royal Navy had saved most of a British army. It had evacuated a total of about 43,000 British soldiers; 17,000 had been killed or captured.

The Battle for Crete

THE GERMANS knew that if they were to take full advantage of the conquest of Greece they must control the Greek island of Crete. There they could establish air bases that would dominate the entire eastern end of the Mediterranean. They began preparations for an attack against the island at once, while the German air force bombed it intensively every day. The Germans did not expect much trouble on Crete because there were only 14,000 Greek soldiers there. They knew the British had no troops available for the defense of the island except the terribly defeated evacuees from Greece.

The British expected an invasion of Crete and so, despite their losses in Greece and Africa, they tried to prepare the island for the expected attack. About 27,000 of the troops that had been rescued from Greece had been left on Crete by the Royal Navy. New equipment was rushed from Egypt, but the men were still very short of supplies when the German attack came on May 20.

The attack took the form of an airborne assault that struck four points on the island at once. The British defense, under New Zealand General Bernard Freyberg, was much stronger than the Germans had expected. Most of the attackers were killed or cap-

PHOTO FROM EUROPEAN

Heraklion, Crete, after Hitler's dive bombers had done their work.

tured the first day, but a few thousand German paratroops had seized the airfield at Maleme and held on to it through the night despite British counterattacks. On the next day more German airborne troops came in, mostly to Maleme, and by nightfall the field was securely in German hands.

That night — May 21-22 — the Royal Navy discovered two large convoys of small vessels filled with German soldiers trying to reach

Crete from Greece under the cover of darkness. The British ships attacked and sank all of the German vessels except for a few that escaped back to Greece.

The Germans made no further efforts to send troops by sea, but they sent more reinforcements by air and intensified their air attacks against the British ground defenses and warships. The Royal Navy suffered such heavy losses from these German air attacks that they had to withdraw from the waters around Crete during daylight hours.

By May 26 the Germans had flown so many troops into Crete that the British realized that they could no longer hold the island. Again, in the face of intense German pressure, the British ships

PHOTO FROM EUROPEAN

Camouflaged German paratroopers in Crete.

PHOTO FROM EUROPEAN

A German Junkers 52 unloading supplies in Crete.

slipped in to shore to take on the exhausted, battered British soldiers. By the night of May 31, the Battle of Crete was over. This was the only important battle in history that had been won entirely by airborne and air-supplied troops without any help from surface forces. In accomplishing this feat the Germans had fought with bravery as great as that of the exhausted, poorly supplied British troops.

The Royal Navy lost several ships and more than 2,000 men in

PHOTO FROM EUROPEAN

Fast little flat-bottomed outboard motor boats like these played an effective role in the German invasion of Crete.

evacuating 16,000 British soldiers. All of the other defending troops were killed or forced to surrender. German losses, too, had been very heavy. Though the exact figures were never revealed, it is known that about 5,000 men were killed, and about 10,000 wounded. There were also very heavy losses in the convoys that had been stopped by the British Navy. The losses were so great that Hitler decided airborne operations were not worth the cost, and he did not train any more airborne soldiers to take the places of those who had been killed or disabled. A few years later he would realize that he had made a terrible mistake.

Hitler Invades Russia

HITLER never carried out his plan to invade Britain. When he sent his *Luftwaffe* on repeated bombing runs to soften the little island for invasion, the Royal Air Force defeated it so badly in the Battle of Britain that the Nazi dictator decided to attack Russia instead. He was certain that once he had defeated Russia, the British would have to surrender.

Early in 1941 Hitler began to assemble an army of nearly 3,000,000 men near the frontiers of Russia. His invasion of the Balkans may have set his plans back by a few weeks, but he did not intend to invade Russia until June, when the roads would be dry.

About 200,000 men of this great invasion army came from the satellite countries of Romania, Bulgaria, and Hungary. The rest were Germans, most of them veterans of the victorious German campaigns in Poland, Flanders, France, and the Balkans. Again Field Marshal von Brauchitsch was in command. In northern Poland an army group under Field Marshal Wilhelm von Leeb was set to drive through the Russian-occupied Baltic States toward Leningrad. In east central Poland Marshal von Bock's army group prepared to make the main German drive toward Moscow. In southern Poland and Hungary Marshal von Rundstedt's army group was ready to sweep through the Ukraine and southern Russia. In addition, Finland was about to re-enter the war against Russia. Marshal Mannerheim planned to lead the Finnish army against Soviet troops and railroad lines in northwestern Russia.

The Germans expected to destroy the main Russian armies in early battles, then capture the industrial and communications centers of Leningrad and Moscow, and Russia's great agricultural region, the Ukraine. Hitler believed the Russians would then make peace. If they did not, he thought the Communist government would be so weakened that it would soon collapse.

The Soviet armies defending Russia's frontiers totaled a little over 3,000,000 men. About 1,000,000 Russian soldiers were scattered elsewhere over the great country, and there were large numbers of trained reserves among the Russian people. Like the German armies, the Russian forces were organized in three army groups. In the Baltic States and northwest Russia was the army group of Marshal Kliment Voroshilov. Marshal Semyon Timoshenko commanded an army group in Russian-held Poland and White Russia. In the Ukraine and south Russia was the group of Marshal Semyon Budenny.

These great armies were about to fight across a tremendous area of the world. From the Arctic to the Black Sea the battle front would stretch over 2,000 miles. And from east to west the struggle would spread over a region 1,700 miles wide. There were very few roads, and these were mostly dirt — dusty in summer, muddy bogs during the fall and spring, and hidden under deep snow in winter. There were endless forests to go through, and broad rivers and two tremendous marshes to cross. The only place that tanks could operate easily was in the grassy plains — or steppes — of the Ukraine.

69

THE GERMAN INVASION OF RUSSIA, 1941-1942

RUSSIAN
WINTER OFFENSIVE
DECEMBER, 1942

EXTENT OF
GERMAN ADVANCE

The German advance rolled forward just as it had in Poland, France, and the Balkans. The Russians were completely unable to stop the *Blitzkrieg* attacks. The Germans were victorious everywhere, but they suffered heavily under the fierce Russian resist-

70

ance. In the first ten weeks they inflicted more than a million casualties on the Russians, but they lost more than 450,000 men themselves.

The Germans now realized that this was a different kind of war than those of the previous years. They were just as successful in winning battles, but they had never had to fight on so large a battlefield. The Russians, even though they were badly cut up, simply fell back, received reinforcements, and began the battle again.

The Germans were discouraged, but they did not stop their attacks. Actually, they were very close to complete success, for the Russians had used up almost all of their available reserves. If the Germans had continued their drive toward Moscow, they would certainly have captured the Russian capital in September or October.

But Hitler was looking at a map in his headquarters in Germany. He saw that Rundstedt and Bock had driven spearheads deep into Russia south and north of Kiev, the capital of the Ukraine. About

A Nazi tank crossing a river in Russia.

PHOTO FROM EUROPEAN

WIDE WORLD PHOTOS

German troops battling snow and wind in the Russian Ukraine.

PHOTO FROM EUROPEAN

"General Mud" helped slow the German advance in Russia.

German mechanized units sometimes proved useless on the great plains of Russia. Then men and horses took over.

1,000,000 Russians under Budenny were holding the central Ukraine between these German spearheads. Hitler ordered his generals to surround Budenny's army group. So, early in September, Bock and Rundstedt halted their advance and, on September 10, began a great encirclement, more than a hundred miles east of the Russian defenders of Kiev.

There were two weeks of desperate fighting before the two German spearheads met in the central Ukraine. About 600,000 Russians were captured, and most of the remainder of Budenny's army group were killed or wounded. The Germans lost only 100,000 men. Though this was a large number, it was small in comparison to the terrible losses they had inflicted on the Russians. But Hitler

WIDE WORLD PHOTOS

This German truck never reached the eastern front.

These Russian factory workers were ready to defend their factory if the Germans approached.

SOVFOTO

had won his battle at the cost of losing the war. He had made his greatest mistake.

If the Germans had pressed on to Moscow, Budenny's army would still have been trapped in the Ukraine. By turning off to the side for several hundred miles of marching and fighting, the Germans had worn out many of their tanks and tank crews. They had no more men or machines to replace these losses. More important, they had lost four to six weeks of good fighting weather. Hitler had been so sure that the war would be a quick one that he had not bothered to gather any equipment or supplies for winter fighting. When the Germans started advancing toward Moscow again, about October 1, winter was coming on fast. Already the weather was getting very cold, and the troops were totally unprepared for it.

Although the Germans had destroyed most of Budenny's army, they had given the Russians time to collect reserves to defend Moscow. Stalin had taken the chief of his general staff, Marshal Georgi Zhukov, and put him in command of the forces defending the Russian capital. And now the fall rains were slowing down the German tanks. Zhukov was being helped by "General Mud."

Even though their tanks and trucks were wearing out after the hard battles and the long marches, the Germans kept pressing forward. At Viasma they surrounded and captured another great force of Russians. Soon afterwards, they did the same thing at Bryansk. By December 5, they had gotten to within fifteen miles of Moscow.

Now the cruel Russian winter closed in. The Russians, who had learned their lesson in the Finnish War, were prepared to fight in cold and snow. The Germans were not. Their advance came to a halt. Without proper winter clothing, many of the soldiers froze to death. Without the right kind of oil and special equipment, the tanks and trucks did not run properly.

Zhukov had been waiting for this moment. He had held out a strong reserve. Now he ordered these troops forward in a great counterattack.

The Germans were actually in the suburbs of Moscow when the Russians struck on December 6. The Germans were thrown back. After being so close to victory, they were now faced with disaster. But they fought on in defense as bravely and skillfully as they had in their attacks. Despite cold and exhaustion, they were able to form a number of strong defensive positions which they called "hedge-hogs." Although the Russians pushed them back for a way, the Germans soon halted their attackers. They spent the rest of the winter deep in Russia.

In the north, the Germans had come very close to capturing Leningrad. With the help of the Finns, they had the city almost completely surrounded for a time. During their counteroffensive

Riflemen of a Russian cavalry unit on the attack in the Mozdok area.

SOVFOTO

Russian soldiers on the alert in the bombed Kharkov area.

SOVFOTO

the Russians managed to re-open the railroad supply route to Leningrad, but the Germans still remained on three sides of the city. The siege of Leningrad continued for another two years.

Although the Finns seized quite a bit of Russian territory north of Leningrad, they were unable to capture the main Russian Arctic seaport of Murmansk. They raided and cut the railroad line from Murmansk to Leningrad, but the Russians built a new railroad to connect Murmansk with Moscow. So the port of Murmansk remained open to receive the great quantities of supplies which the British, at the price of terrible losses in ships and men, immediately sent by sea to their hard-pressed Russian allies.

Stalingrad and the German Retreat

AFTER the Germans stopped the Russian winter counteroffensive, both sides worked hard to recover from the terrible fighting of the preceding summer, fall, and winter. By spring 1942 both armies were in better shape. The Russians, in particular, had improved. They had learned a great deal from the Germans. Hitler's soldiers, however, though they were weaker than they had been in 1941, were still far better than the more numerous Russian armies. When, in May, the Germans easily defeated a Russian drive near Kharkov, Stalin realized that he would have to stay on the defensive and try to hold off the expected German attacks.

At this time Hitler was planning two offensives. The first was small in area, but important to the Germans. In 1941 they had captured all of the Crimean peninsula except for Sevastopol — the largest city of the Crimea, and the most important seaport of the Black Sea. If they could capture Sevastopol, Hitler would have complete control over the Black Sea. The attack began on June 7, 1942. It was the beginning of a terrible four-week struggle in which the Germans were completely victorious by July 2.

Hitler's other planned offensive was tremendous in area, and important to both the Germans and Russians. He planned to have his armies strike eastward across southern Russia to the Caucasus and the Russian oil fields at Baku. Without oil, the Russians would not be able to move their tanks, trucks, planes, or guns. And Germany was in desperate need of the oil. Furthermore, an advance in this region of southern Russia would deprive the Russians of their last remaining important agricultural area. Without wheat, the Russian people would be close to starvation.

But Hitler had made two more mistakes that would seriously interfere with his plans.

In the first place, many of the Russians in the region overrun by the Germans had been tired of Stalin's Communist dictatorship before the war began. If the Germans had treated them well, most of them would have become their loyal allies and supporters. But the German Nazis that Hitler sent to rule the newly conquered provinces treated the Ukrainian and Russian inhabitants as badly as, or even worse than, the Communists had done. The people in these regions decided that they would rather be ruled by tyrannical Russian Communists than by German Nazis. And so they began to fight against their conquerors. They destroyed railroads, shot German soldiers, and forced the Germans to keep large numbers of troops controlling the rear areas instead of using them on the fighting front.

Hitler's second mistake at this time was in making a plan for a move to the Caucasus that would extend the German battle line to nearly 3,000 miles in length. The Germans did not have enough men to hold such a line. With the strongest forces of their army driving to the southeast, the thin German lines in central Russia could easily be cut by the main Russian armies. And the Russian soldiers could count on a great deal of help from the peasants fighting the Germans behind the German lines.

Hitler's staff had recommended that he continue eastward to Moscow and Kazan, thus defeating the main Russian armies and cutting the railroad lines to south Russia. He could then have taken Baku and the southern wheat fields later, without danger of

THE RUSSO-GERMAN FRONT, 1942-1943

ARCTIC OCEAN

MURMANSK

NORWAY

SWEDEN

FINLAND

BALTIC SEA

LENINGRAD

VON PAULUS ARMY

DON R.

VOLGA R.

EXTENT OF GERMAN ADVANCE STALINGRAD

BATTLE OF STALINGRAD

Volga R. KAZAN

RUSSIAN COUNTEROFFENSIVE WINTER 1943

MOSCOW

VIASMA

U. S. S. R.

White Russia

SMOLENSK

BRYANSK

EXTENT OF GERMAN ADVANCE SUMMER 1943

GERMANY

POLAND

KIEV

Ukraine

KHARKOV

Donets R. Don R.

STALINGRAD

ROSTOV

CASPIAN SEA

Dnieper R.

HUNGARY

ODESSA

Crimea

SEVASTOPOL

RUMANIA

YUGOSLAVIA

BULGARIA

BAKU

Caucasus Mts.

BLACK SEA

ITALY

TURKEY

a Russian attack against an exposed German flank. But Hitler
would not listen to his generals. He now considered himself a
military genius, and he thought his generals were too timid.

When the German attack began on June 28, 1942, it was almost

81

as successful as it had been a year earlier. Within a month the German front in the south had been advanced by three hundred miles, and the drive to the southeast continued without delay.

But as the left flank of the great German advance approached the Volga River, near Stalingrad, it ran into intensified Russian resistance. Stalin recognized Hitler's mistake, and he knew that if he could hold the Volga River line he would be in a position to cut off the German spearheads farther south.

Hitler was infuriated by the slow progress near Stalingrad and ordered that the city be taken immediately. But the Germans had stretched their lines too thin to make a strong effort both at Stalingrad and in the advance to the southeast. As a result of Hitler's order, neither attack was as strong as it could or should have been. The German drive to the Caucasus was slowed down, while the German attacks at Stalingrad were repulsed. By November the Germans were halted everywhere. They had almost, but not quite, reached the Baku oil fields. They had almost, but not quite, captured Stalingrad.

Now the Russians took advantage of the dangerously exposed situation of the German army. On November 19 they struck the German lines south and north of Stalingrad, employing the same kind of infantry-armor penetrations the Germans had used so well in Poland, Flanders, France, the Balkans, and Russia. The Germans had taught the Russians how to make war, and the Russians had learned well. In four days they had surrounded an entire German army in front of Stalingrad.

General Friedrich von Paulus, who commanded the encircled German army, prepared to fight his way out of the trap. He could have done so with some hard fighting, but he received orders from Hitler to stay where he was and not to retreat an inch. Paulus obeyed the order. The encirclement grew tighter and stronger as the Russians advanced steadily westward through the entire weakened German line. The German spearheads in the Caucasus, south of Stalingrad, barely escaped capture.

By February 2, General von Paulus had to surrender the remnants of his starving, surrounded army. The Russians were still advancing westward, first across the Don, then across the Donets River.

In March the Russian offensive was halted at Kharkov by a brilliant counterattack led by Marshal Erich von Manstein. In the way in which he organized the defeated German troops, then led them in this counterattack, Manstein proved himself to be one of the greatest generals of World War II.

The improvement in the Russian fighting qualities in the eighteen months since midsummer of 1941 had been tremendous. But the credit goes not only to the tough Russian fighting men and the leaders who had taught them to fight the German way. Much of the improvement was due to the new equipment that the Russians were receiving in great quantity from the United States and Britain. By the spring of 1943 the Russians had received from the United States more than 3,000 airplanes, 2,400 tanks, 80,000 trucks, and all kinds of other supplies. They had gotten almost as much from the British.

During the spring of 1943 the Russians kept up the pressure against the Germans, and pushed them steadily back in central and south Russia. By the end of the year the front ran along the line of the Dnieper River. Although the Germans still held a huge chunk of Russian territory, they were completely on the defensive in the east. There seemed little prospect of any real German victory over Russia.

83

The United States and the War in Europe, 1942-1943

THE JAPANESE attack on Pearl Harbor, December 7, 1941, had had no immediate effect on the war in Europe. At least so it seemed to the people who were fighting the war, or to the countries that had been overrun by the Nazis. This was because the United States did not yet have the soldiers or the equipment to start any important war operations.

Shortly after the attack on Pearl Harbor, Churchill and his military advisers met with President Roosevelt and the senior American military men in Washington. At this meeting a number of decisions were made that shaped the course of the remainder of the war.

The immediate problem was to make sure that the Axis — Germany, Italy, and Japan — would not win the war before the United States was fully ready to fight. The American Army, Navy, and Air Force must be built up, and American industry must have time to turn out the equipment needed for American fighting men.

The United States and British leaders agreed that Germany was the most dangerous enemy. They therefore decided that Hitler must be defeated before the full might of the Allies was turned against Japan. Many Americans did not agree with this decision. They thought Japan should be punished immediately for its treacherous attack on Pearl Harbor. Actually, there was no choice. A powerful navy was necessary for an attack on Japan, and the United States Navy had been gravely crippled by the Pearl Harbor attack. Furthermore, there was a danger that if the Allies did not put immediate pressure on Germany, Russia might be completely knocked out of the war. This might have meant that Hitler would become too strong to be defeated.

The next decision that Roosevelt and Churchill and their military advisers reached was to create a command organization to run a war that had spread over the entire globe. This organization was called the Combined Chiefs of Staff. It included the top military men of Britain and the United States. The British members were called the Chiefs of Staff Committee, and the American members were called the Joint Chiefs of Staff.

The British and American Chiefs of Staff kept in constant touch with each other and met frequently in 1942 and 1943. For much of that time the outlook was gloomy. The low point was in the summer of 1942, when the Germans in Russia were driving on to Stalingrad and the Caucasus, while at the same time General Rommel, in Africa, was marching across northern Egypt toward Alexandria and the Suez Canal. The Japanese had overrun all of the Western Pacific and Southeast Asia, and were threatening India, Australia, and Alaska. It looked as though the two German spearheads would unite in Turkey or Iran and then push on eastward to meet the Japanese in India. German submarines were sinking American and British merchant ships so fast that it seemed very likely they might starve Britain into submission and prevent America from sending an army across the ocean.

By the end of 1943 things looked better. The Germans had been pushed back in Russia. The Americans and British had driven

BIRNBACK PUBLISHING SERVICE

Germans mounted this great revolving gun on the French coast.

Rommel out of Africa, had captured Sicily, had knocked Italy out of the war, and were fighting the Germans in southern Italy. In the Pacific, the Americans had driven the Japanese from most of the Solomon Islands and from their Aleutian Island strongholds on Kiska and Attu. American and Chinese troops had started an invasion in north Burma.

Promising as the Allied picture looked, however, there was much that made the Combined Chiefs of Staff sober indeed about the future. The Germans still held practically all of Europe, and their tenacious defense in Italy and Russia made many people wonder if they would ever be driven back to Germany. Meanwhile, Hitler had made threats about a "secret weapon." The Allies knew that he was referring to a powerful long-range missile with which he could attack England from France and the Low Countries. The question was: Could Britain continue the war under a hail of missiles such as these?

On Tarawa, the Japanese had proven that they could inflict a terrible toll on attackers trying to recapture their island strongholds. Many people doubted that the Americans could stand these tremendous losses for every Japanese-held island in the Pacific. The Japanese, moreover, had advanced so far into China that they threatened to knock that country out of the war. This would release another million trained Japanese fighting men to hold Japan's far-flung Asiatic and Pacific possessions.

It was true that the Allies had halted or slowed down the wave of Axis conquest. But could they defeat the Axis? If Germany and Japan could hold on to even half the areas they had conquered, history's judgment might be that the Allies had lost the war.

Index

Eben Emael, Fort, 39
Egypt, 54, 85
England. *See* Great Britain
English Channel, 25, 40, 42
Estonia, 21
Ethiopia, 4

Falkenhorst, General Nikolaus von, 27
Finland, 21; Gulf of, 21, 22, 24; Russian attack on, 22; re-enters war, 69, 77
Finnish army, 22, 24, 77-78
Flanders, 42, 43, 47
France: unprepared for war, 5-7, 20; signs Munich Agreement, 6; enters war, 18; Battle of (*1940*), 47-48; surrender of, 49-50
French armored divisions, 35, 41
French army, 35, 39-43, 45-46, 47-48
Freyberg, General Bernard, 62

Gamelin, General Maurice, 35, 39, 43
German air force. *See* Luftwaffe
German armored divisions: in Poland, 10, 13, 16; in France, Belgium, Holland (*1940*), 34, 39, 42, 47-48; in Greece, 60; in Russia, 76
German army: in Poland, 10, 13, 15-16; in invasion of Scandinavia, 27, 29-30; grouping of, on Western front, 34; in France, Belgium, Holland (*1940*), 38-44, 47-48; in Balkans, 56, 58-60; on Crete, 62-65; grouping of, for attack on Russia, 68-69; advance of, in Russia, 70-71, 74, 76, 79, 81-82; in Russian winter, 76-77; retreat of, in Russia, 83, 85, 87; in Italy, 87
Germany: prepares for war, 1, 4; pre-war aggressions of, 2, 4, 6, 7; between the two World Wars, 3-4; signs treaty with Russia (*1939*), 8, 21; invades Poland, 10; invades Scandinavia, 25, 27-30, 33; invades France, Belgium, Holland, 37-39; attacks Greece and Yugoslavia, 56, 58-60; invades Russia, 70-71; Allies concentrate on defeat of, 84-85
Gort, Lord, General, 35
Great Britain: unprepared for war, 5-7, 20; signs Munich Agreement, 6; guarantees Poland's freedom, 8, 18; enters war, 18; intends to mine Norwegian coast, 27, 28-29; bombing of, 27, 68, 87; awaits German invasion 51-52, 68; sends supplies to Russia, 78, 83; cooperation of, with U.S., 84-85
Greece: Italian attack on, 54; German attack on, 56, 58-60; evacuation of British troops from, 60, 62
Greek army, 54-55, 60, 62

Haakon, King of Norway, 29, 33
Hel, 16
Helsinki, 22
Hitler, Adolf, 21, 50, 87; political goals of, 1-2; pre-war acts of, 2-7, 8; starts war, 8, 10; and Scandinavian campaign, 25, 27, 33; and invasion of France, Belgium, Holland, 34, 44; military mistakes of, 44, 67, 76, 80-81; plans to invade Britain, 51, 68; and Balkans campaign, 56; plans to attack Russia, 56, 58, 68-69; and Russian campaign, 71, 74, 76, 79-82
Holland: neutrality of, 35; invasion of, 37-39
Hungary, 56, 58, 68

Invasion plans, German: of Scandinavia, 27; of Low Countries and France, 34, 37; of Britain, 51, 68; of Russia, 68-69
Italian army: in France, 48; in Greece and Albania, 54-55, 60
Italy: under Mussolini, 4; pre-war aggressions of, 4, 7; enters war, 48; attacks Greece, 54; defeat of, 87; war in, 87

Japan, 4, 84-85, 87
Joint Chiefs of Staff, 85

Karelian Isthmus, 22, 24
Kazan, 80
Kharkov, 79, 83
Kiev, 71, 74
Kiska, 87
Kock, 16
Kristiansand, 27
Kutno, 15

Ladoga, Lake, 22, 24
Latvia, 21

21-22; and war in Russia, 76, 79, 82
Stalingrad, 82-83, 85
Stavanger, 27
Submarines, German, 85
Sudetenland, 3, 6, 7
Suez Canal, 85
Suomussalmi, 24

Tanks. *See* German armored divisions, etc.
Tarawa, 87
The Hague, 37
Thermopylae, Pass of, 60
Timoshenko, Marshal Semyon, 69
Trondheim, 27, 30, 33

Ukraine, 69, 71, 74, 76
United States, 84-85, 87; sends aid to
    Russia, 83

Versailles, Treaty of, 3-4, 7
Viasma, 76
Vichy Government, 50
Viipuri, 22
Visconti-Prasca, General, 54
Volga River, 82
Voroshilov, Marshal Kliment, 69

Warsaw, 13, 15, 16, 56
Westwall. See Siegfried Line
Weygand, General Maxime, 43, 47, 48
Wilhelmina, Queen, 38
Wilson, General Henery, 56, 60
World War I, 2, 3, 50

Yugoslavia, 56, 58, 59

Zhukov, Marshal Georgi, 76-77